SQUIGGLE!

by
Kenzô Hayashi

Workman Publishing
New York

Hitofudegaki Dôbutsu Zukan
Illustrations copyright © 2011 by Kenzô Hayashi
First published in Japan in 2011 by Child Honsha Co., Ltd., Tokyo
English translation rights arranged with Child Honsha Co., Ltd.
through Japan Foreign-Rights Centre

Library of Congress Cataloging-in-Publication Data is available.

ISBN 978-1-5235-0109-0

Illustrator Kenzô Hayashi
Designer Tim Hall
Editor Nathalie Le Du
Production Editor Amanda Hong
Production Manager Doug Wolff

Workman books are available at special discounts when purchased in bulk for
premiums and sales promotions as well as for fund-raising or educational use.
Special editions or book excerpts can also be created to specification.
For details, contact the Special Sales Director at the address below,
or send an email to specialmarkets@workman.com.

Workman Publishing Co., Inc.
225 Varick Street
New York, NY 10014-4381

workman.com

WORKMAN is a registered trademark of Workman Publishing Co., Inc.

Printed in China
First printing August 2017

10 9 8 7 6 5 4 3 2 1

Every masterpiece begins with one line…

This book shows you how to use a simple line to draw animals from all over the world.

We call it
SQUIGGLING!

Grab a pencil, pen, crayon, or marker, and start by tracing the animal on the sketch pad. You can start at either end of the line.

Just keep your writing utensil on the paper the whole time.

Then, try it again freehand.

Besides that, there's no right or wrong way to squiggle.

You can even go wild and invent your own squiggle.

And remember—a squiggle doesn't have to be perfect to be wonderful.

Love your squiggle?
Why not share it? You can tear your masterpiece off the sketch pad and give it to a parent or friend, tape it to a notebook, frame it, or simply put it on your fridge.

When you're done with the sketch pad, fold the cover over to make book flaps.

Then you can always come back to squiggle some more.

Now let's see where the line leads you!

Mouse

9

Rabbit

Snake

Sheep

Rooster, Chicken, and Chick

Dog

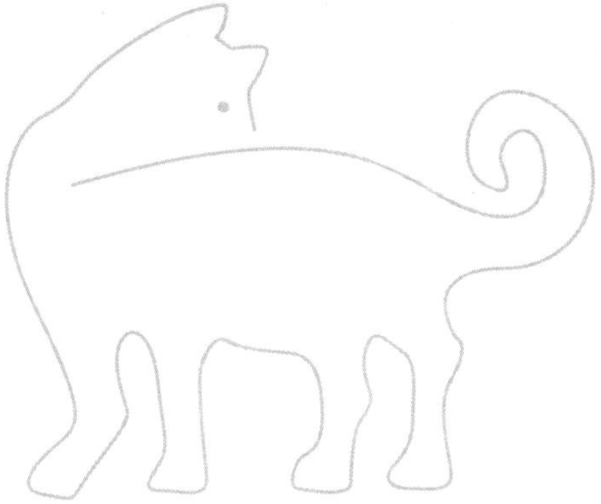

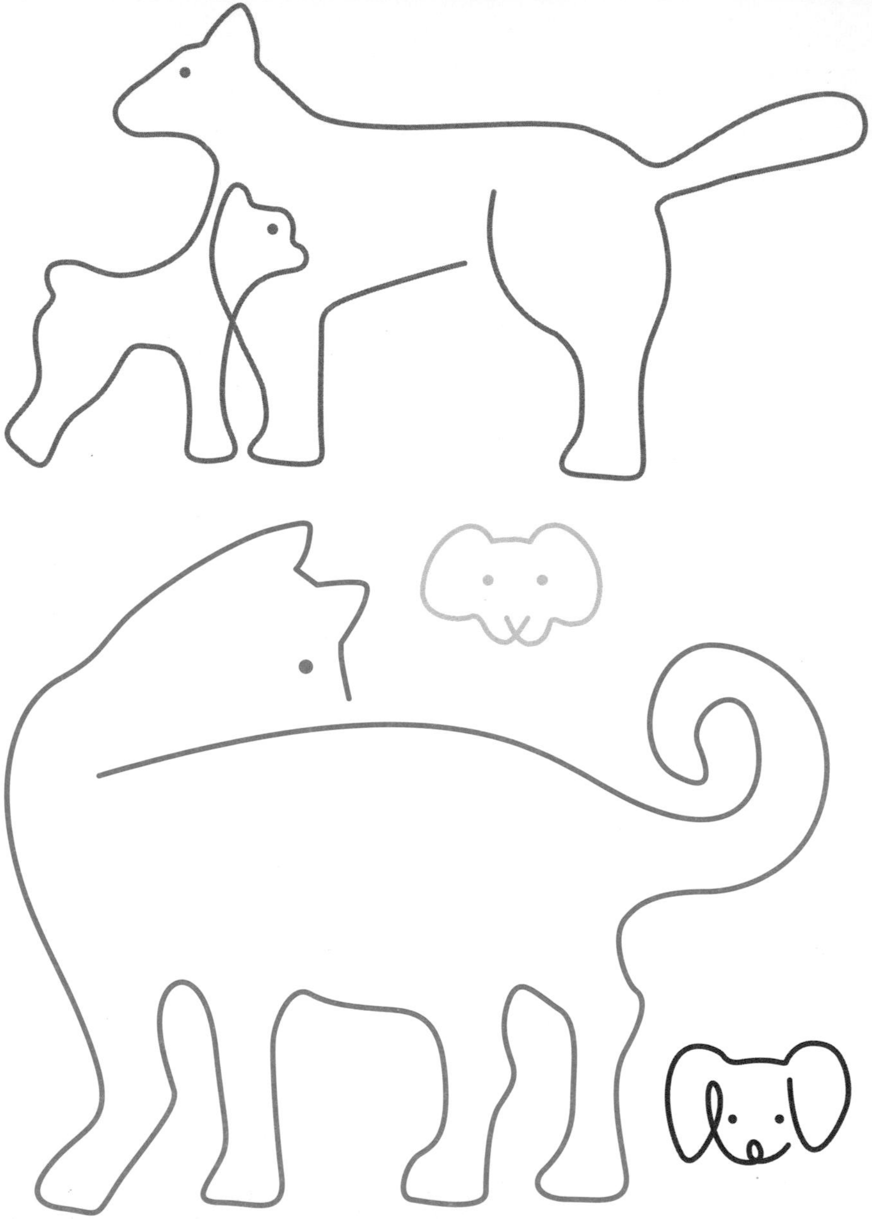

Fox

Bat

Cat

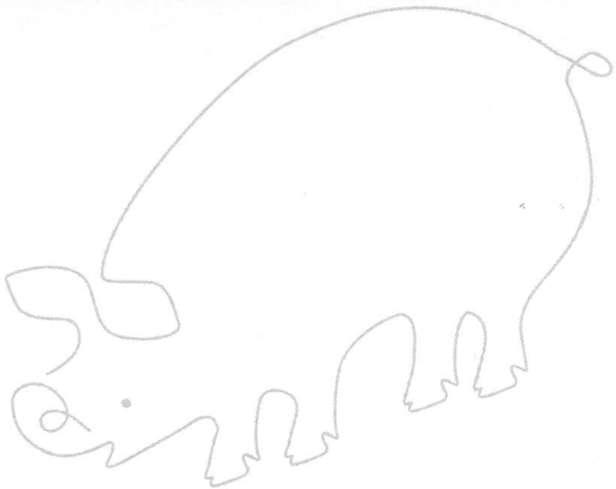

Pig

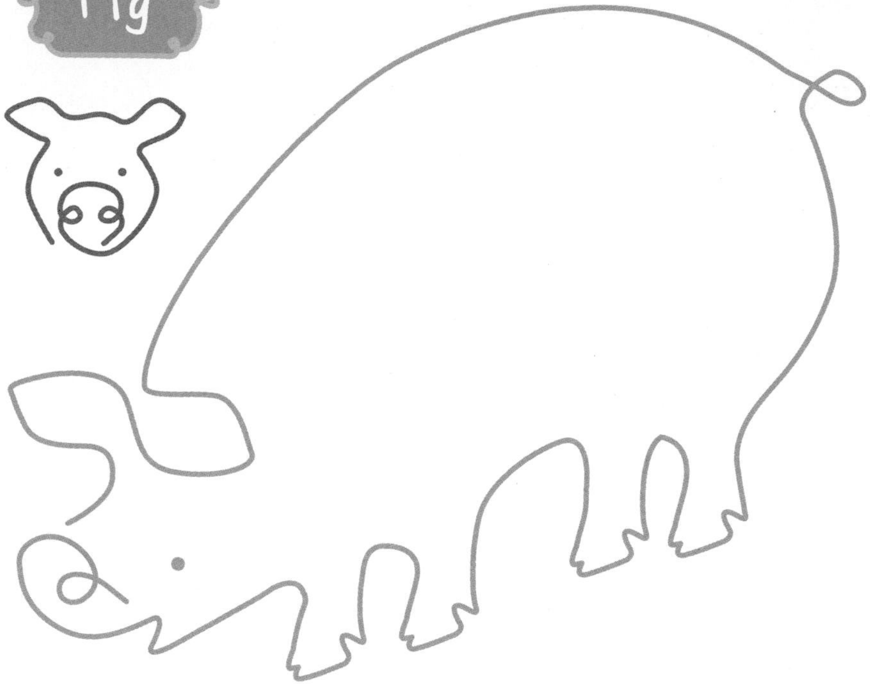

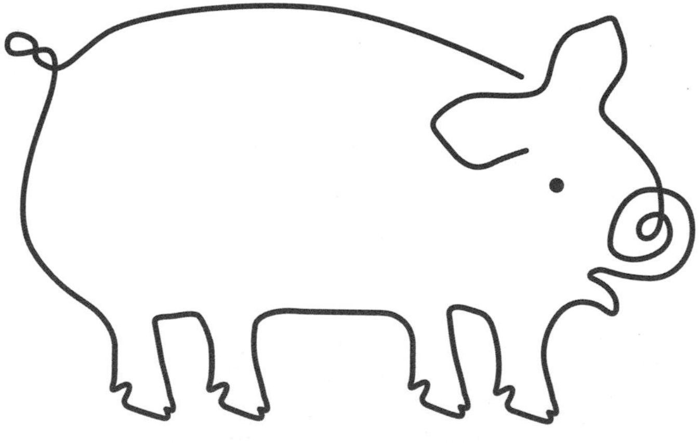

Tiger

Monkey

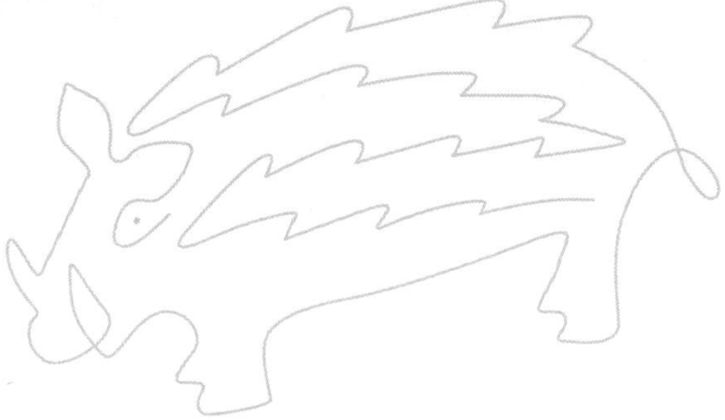

Boar

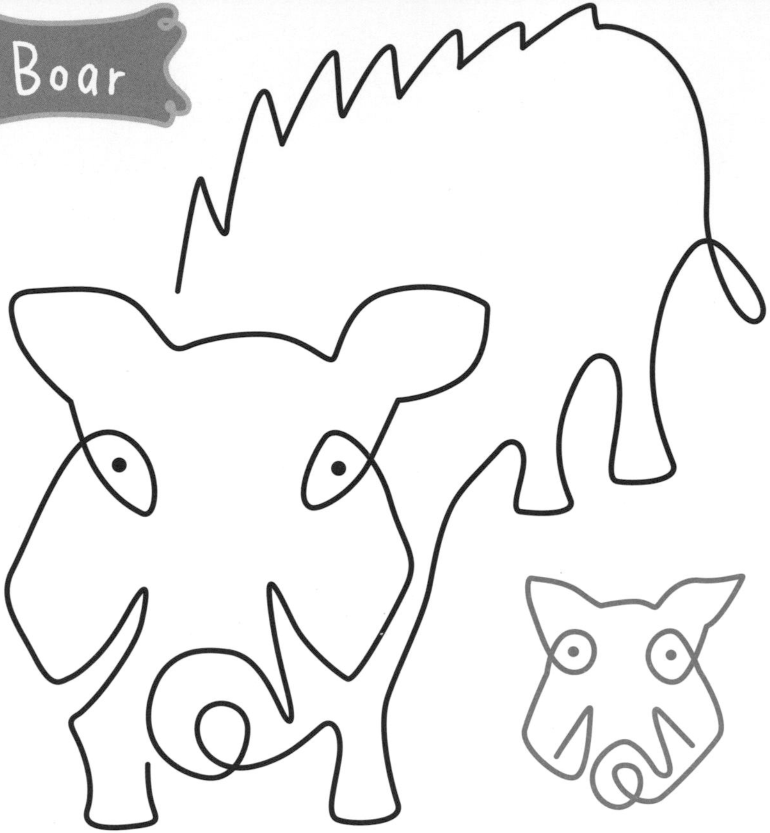

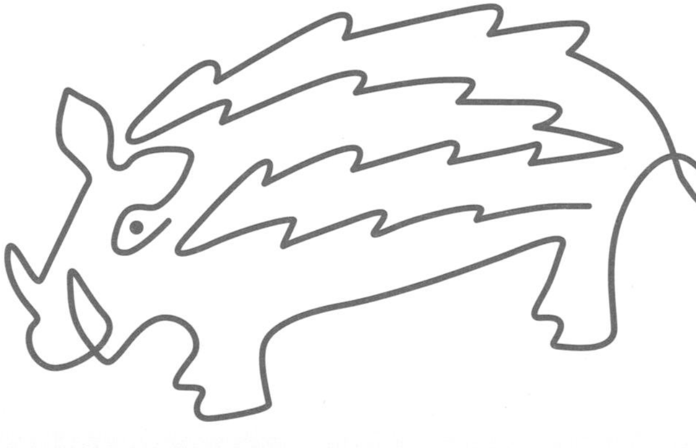

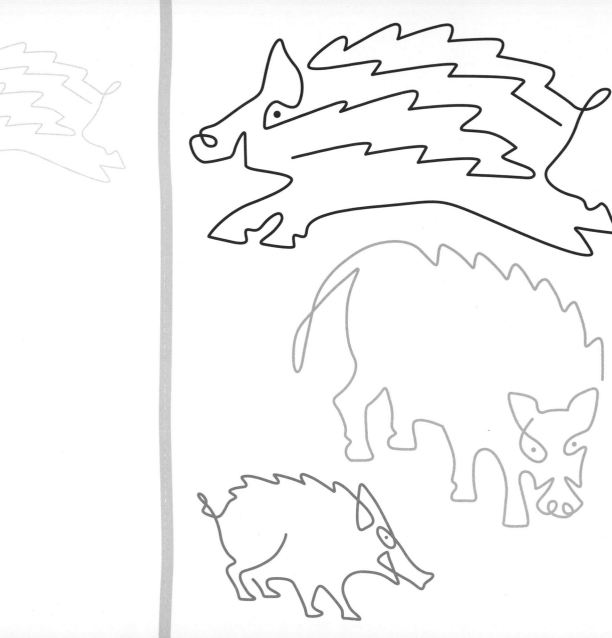

Elephant

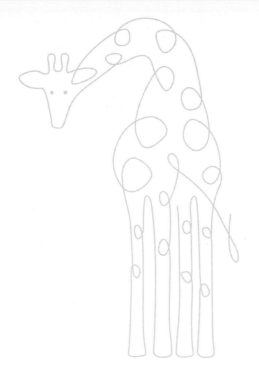

Giraffe

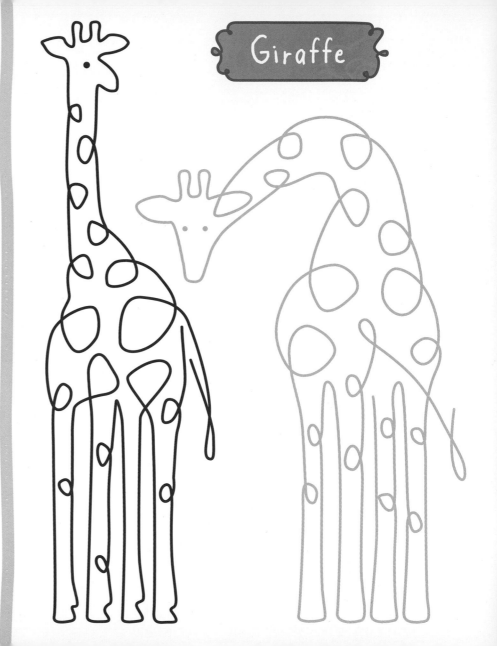

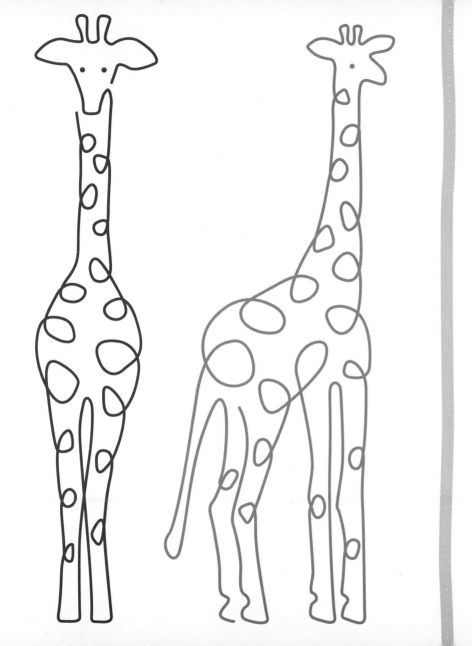

Camel

Zebra

Buffalo

Crocodile

Tapir

Wolf

Panda

Kangaroo

Chameleon

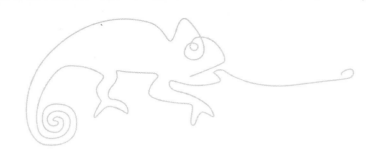

Seahorse

Whale

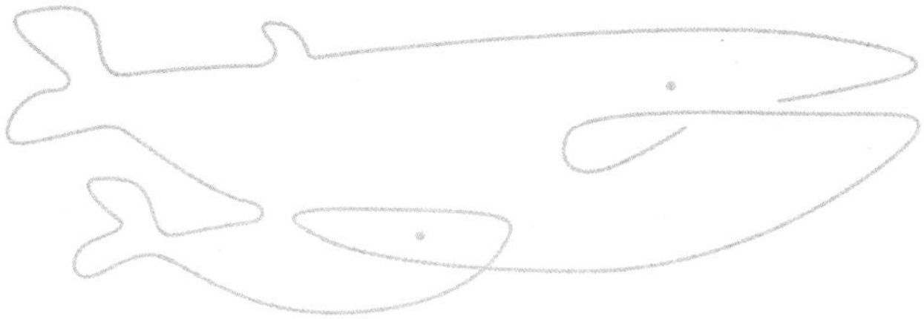

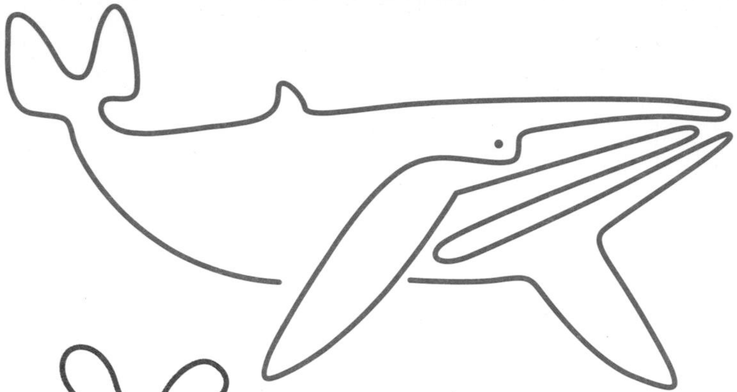

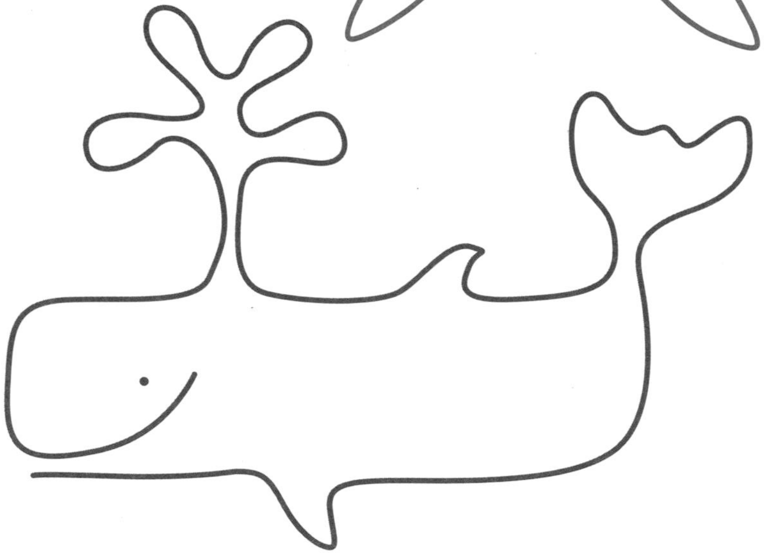

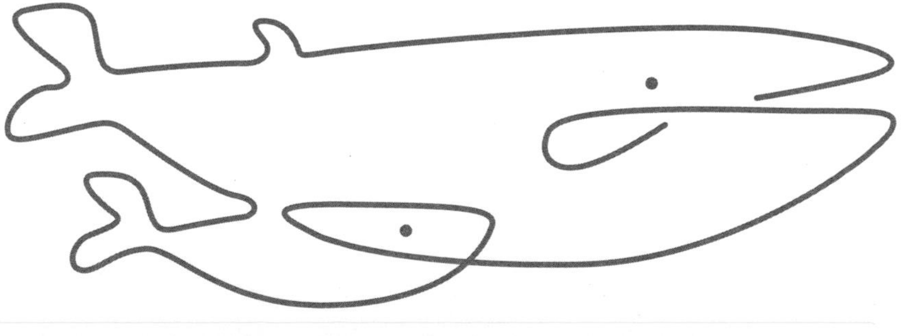

Dolphin

Polar Bear

Manatee

Seal

Sea Lion

Seagull

Fish

Sunfish

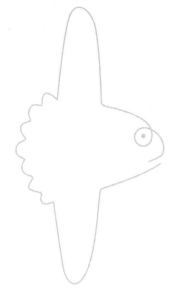

Shark

Flat Fish

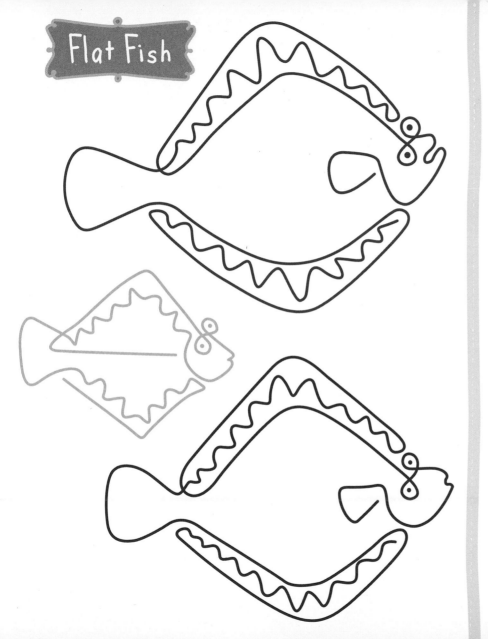
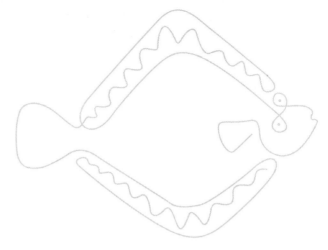

Goldfish

Lobster

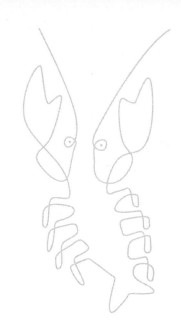

Squid

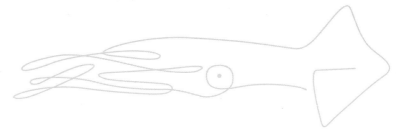

Crab

Clam, Mollusk, and Starfish

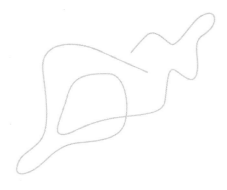

Snail

Cicada

Grasshopper

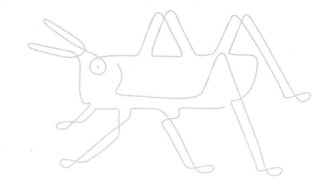

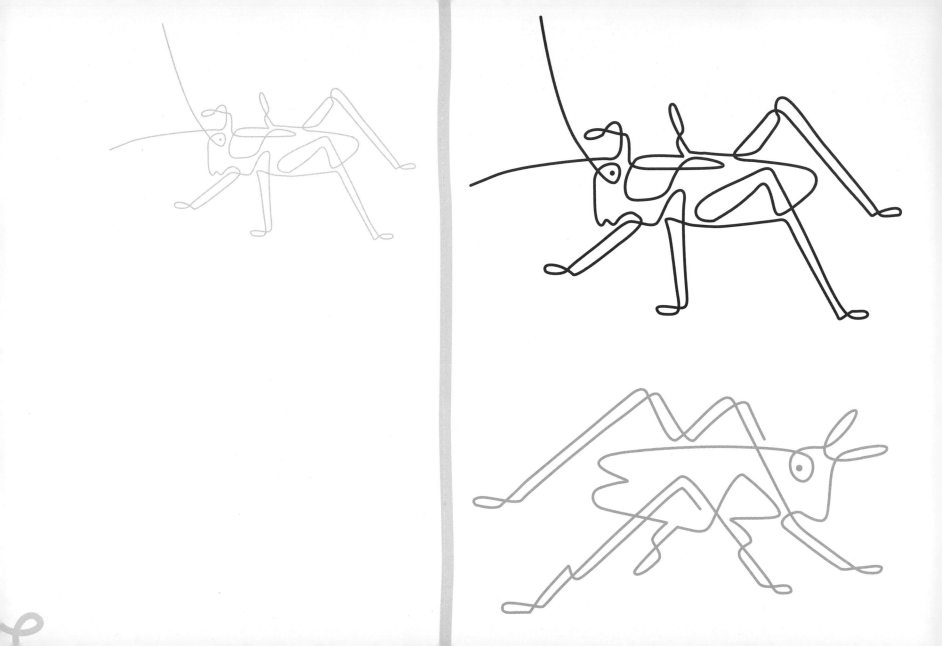

Ant

Dragonfly

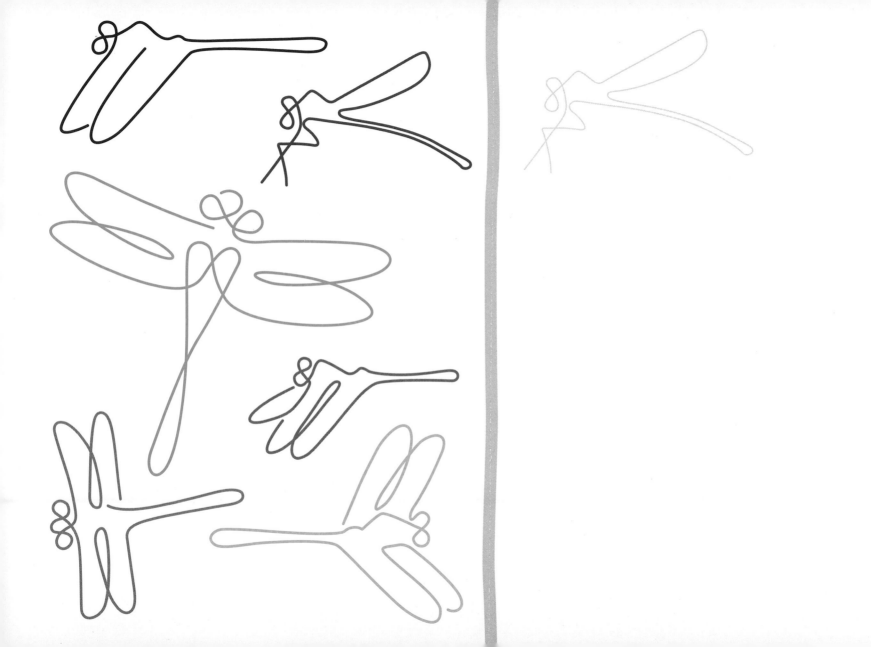

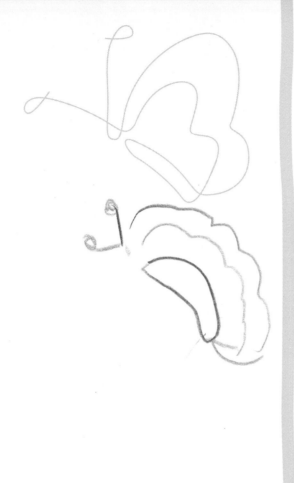

Ladybug

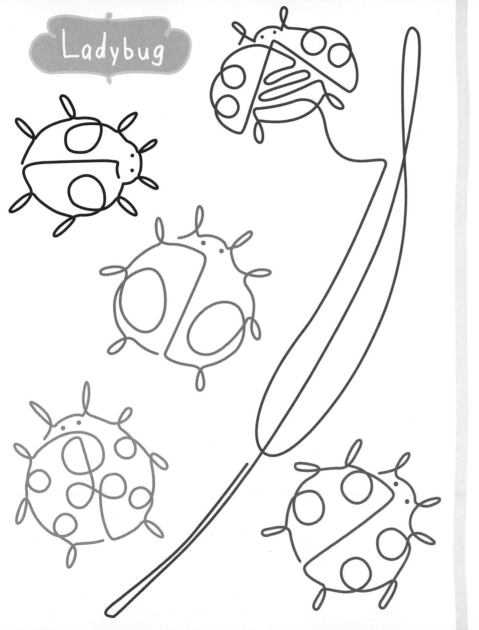

Pelican

Ostrich

Owl

Pigeon

Swan

Crane

Goose

Green Pheasant

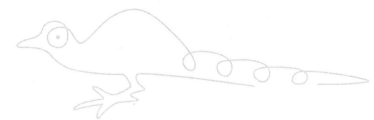

Falcon

Lyla amaBella
Tipton
Sister

The End